EXPECTING...
IS THERE NO KING IN YOU

Expecting...
Is There No King In You

Chiquita S. Holmes

Copyright © 2024 by Chiquita S. Holmes

All rights reserved. No part of this publication may be reproduced, distributed, or transmitted in any form or by any means, including photocopying, recording, or other electronic or mechanical methods, without the prior written permission of the copyright owner and the publisher, except in the case of brief quotations embodied in critical reviews and certain other noncommercial uses permitted by copyright law. For permission requests, write to the publisher, addressed "Attention: Permissions Coordinator," at the address below.

CITIOFBOOKS, INC.
3736 Eubank NE Suite A1
Albuquerque, NM 87111-3579
www.citiofbooks.com
Hotline: 1 (877) 389-2759
Fax: 1 (505) 930-7244

Ordering Information:

Quantity sales. Special discounts are available on quantity purchases by corporations, associations, and others. For details, contact the publisher at the address above.

Printed in the United States of America.

ISBN-13: Hardback 978-1-962366-44-1

Library of Congress Control Number: 2023918398

Table of Contents

Dedication iii

1. Why is Jesus so Important?...................................1

2. The Bible Really Speaks 3

3. Time Doesn't Exist For You 5

4. Warriors Of God Must Speak.................................7

5. Why Am I Listening For God's Voice 9

6. God Takes The Foolish Things.............................11

7. He Sent His Angels 13

8. As He Is So Am I...16

9. Praise Is A Weapon..18

10. What Is Your Confession?? 20

11. Your Scars Have Become Beauty 22

12. I Kissed You This Morning.................................24

13. When God Whispers 26

14. A Hurt That Only God Almighty Knows 28

15. To Be Blessed 30

16. Power of His Name 32

17. Without A Cause 34

18. Why should the Meek Inherit 36

19. What Happened At The Cross...38

20. Responses To The Finished Works 40

21. I Am A Witness..42

22. It Is Finished 44

23. What is Prayer?? 46

24. Why Should I Pour Out My Heart To The Lord 48

25. What Does It Look Like to Operate in the Finished Works 50

Dedication

I would like to dedicate this book to My Source and some very important people In my life.

I have to give thanks, all the praise and honor to the Lord Jesus Christ, who not

only has shown me that He is real, but also amazes me by letting me see and

And understand how powerful He truly is.

To my wonderful and hard working mom Cynthia, who was also my best

Friend here on Earth. I could talk to her about anything… I miss you dearly

To my two precious children Savon and Royalty, who always keep me on my Toes.

And last but certainly not least, to my husband Terence who always goes above

And beyond for me. I am so glad we found each other. You are God's gift to me.

Why is Jesus so Important?

Father God asks Mankind, "Do you really want to know Me?"
"Do you really want to experience My Presence?"
Then I'll tell you what I will do
I will send you My Son.
His name shall be called "God is with Us."
He is the very essence and xpression of Me because we are one.

When you get to know Him, then you will know Me.
When you hear Him speak, it will be my words that He tells you, coming from my heart.
This is the way I will present Myself to Mankind.
This is the way it is settled in heaven on this day, and it will never change.

Scriptures clearly state: "To know the Father, you must go through the Son,
Kiss the Son lest the Father be angry."
But be careful that you do not ignore Him or mistreat the things He tells you,
Because if you do, it is as if you are mistreating and ignoring Me because I have sent Him to represent Me.

This is my passion for your lives, to set mankind free from all bondage.
Choose my Son Jesus and you will never be ashamed for believing in Him.
The Father is waiting, your destiny is already written.
Jesus is important to you because God gave you His very best.
He gave you His heart
He gave you His Son to help you navigate the victory He has already won for you.

How can you resist such an offer, how can you resist the Great I Am…
The God of the Universe invites you to accept His invitation of graciousness,
and become more than you have ever dreamed you could be.
This choice has always been yours.

The Bible Really Speaks

It is said that a picture is worth a thousand words,
but what about a book like no other?
That has no pictures,
but every time you read it, the meaning changes.

Each word begins to speak directly to you,
the more and more time you spend reading it.
This book will capture and command your heart's attention if you allow it to.

This book called the Bible speaks riddles, enigmas, and mysteries,
that only God Himself by the Power of the Holy Spirit can unlock for you to understand.
If you believe "Who He says He is" and What He says He can do through you.
It will change your whole attitude and outlook on life without you even recognizing it.
You won't even know you have changed until something out of the ordinary happens to you and your response are unique and different, it will amaze you.

When you read the Bible,
you are actually spending time with God in His Presence.
And remember it is said in any relationship,
the weaker personality will take on the characteristic traits of the stronger personality.

When you are consistently reading the Word of God,
you have begun a relationship with Him.
You now will begin to see the Eternal truth about life,
through His Eyes of Wisdom.
And here you are thinking you were just reading a mere Book,
And it changed your life.

<u>Time Doesn't Exist For You</u>

It's no wonder the promises of God have not sprung forth in your life yet
You need to change your way of thinking.
The manifestation of God's Word doesn't need time.
Faith in God and His Word operates by truth, not time.

Almighty God has given you multiple gifts through one divine exchange at the Cross
The choice has always been yours
To merely exist or to thrive in this life
Renew your mind to the truth
There is no time in the spirit realm
It Is Finished

You must not forget this one thing
It's very important.
With the Lord, a day is like a thousand years,
and a thousand years is like a day.

So, I charge you this day to live knowing
Our God has gone before us

And He is our rear guard
We always win
We always triumph through Christ Jesus

Have confident expectations of His goodness to you
Time doesn't exist for you,
you have already won the victory in life
you just need to hear His strategy
His plan that He has for you

This lie has just been exposed
Now rise up in courage and get your inheritance.

WARRIORS **O**F **G**OD **M**UST **S**PEAK

I have found a great fault in you.
You don't believe a Word I say,
and even when you do (you judge My Word based on what you think you know).
Is the earth's time more than eternity or is it the other way around?

I have no beginning and no ending.
I have no father or mother.
I Am Who I Am.
I Am God alone, Your Unseen Partner.

There is not one thing that happens on the earth that I don't know about.
I made the element you call time and placed you in it.
Yet from the beginning of time,
I have told you to guard your heart because out of it flows the issues of life.

I have given you great power, and that power is released every time you utter a word from your lips.

But can you tell Me what the issues of life are?
Let Me teach you all things, I will always tell you the truth. I will always honor My Word. I will always lead you down a path full of light.

I want nothing more than for you to know Me and imitate My Ways,
yet you are so consumed with doing everything else in a run-of-a day but spending quality time with Me.
Time with Me will make you bold.

Your faith in Me will increase.
You will say to the mountain be removed and it will move.
You can speak to whatever negative circumstance you are in,
and it will change according to My Word and according to your faith in Me.

Then you will glorify My Name here on earth,
and all the nations will begin to believe in Me,
and know they can trust Me to be good to them just as I AM good to you.
But you must first get to really know Me, sit here in My Presence and you will exchange your own will for My Will.

As a believer in Me you are now a Warrior, a King, and a Fighter of justice.
A warrior of God must fight the "Good Fight" and will change the world,
A warrior will decree a thing and fight for justice by
Speaking the truth
God Says You Will Be Heard.

W̲h̲y̲ ̲A̲m̲ ̲I̲ ̲L̲i̲s̲t̲e̲n̲i̲n̲g̲ ̲F̲o̲r̲ ̲G̲o̲d̲'̲s̲ ̲V̲o̲i̲c̲e̲

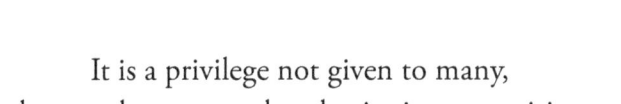

It is a privilege not given to many,
to hear such power and authority in your spirit can
overwhelm you but can be joyous at the same time.
To have a knowing in your inner man of what the world cannot
comprehend
or give attention to.

The Voice of the Lord is majestic,
like many waters or as a thunderous roar,
but as gentle as a small voice to the Believer.
Come closer to Me He says and I will trust you with eternal truth,
which are My secrets that I only reveal to those who long to know
Me and do My Will.

They shall be called My Sons no longer a child,
because you have matured in your relationship with Me,
and all creation is eagerly waiting for you to manifest.

The Lord says whatever I tell you in the dark, speak in the light,
and what you hear whispered in your ear, proclaim it publicly.
And when you speak and release My

Word that I have given you in faith,
Now you will be prophesying of Me.

I AM the Light that shines in the dark,
I AM the Ancient of Days,
I AM The Eternal Wise God there is none like Me,
but if you never ask Me to prepare
your heart to hear from Me as a believer,
then all My Power as Awesome as it is
will remain in Heaven with Me.
So, you be the judge in this matter.
Do you think it is important to hear from Me
On a daily basis with all you see going on in the world today?
I will let you be the judge of that.

G̲o̲d̲ ̲T̲a̲k̲e̲s̲ ̲T̲h̲e̲ ̲F̲o̲o̲l̲i̲s̲h̲ ̲T̲h̲i̲n̲g̲s̲

As foolish as it may seem to the natural man,
You can give and it shall be given unto you,
You can bless those who curse you,
Love your enemies, and pray for those who
despitefully misuse you.

Your thoughts and behavior can imitate your
Heavenly Father as Jesus demonstrated.
The Holy Spirit will deliver the power
you need to overcome any obstacle.
He will only speak to the Believer what
He hears from Heaven.
So much of your new life as a Believer relies on hearing,
From Jesus' .. Hearing His voice is how
the Greatness in you will arise and you will
become a blessing to the world, a witness that Jesus is alive and
hearing is how you will manifest your divine
inheritance to show how well your Father in Heaven
Takes care of you.

When you learn to open the gates of your heart and let Jesus come in, the real you will emerge as a new creation in Christ.
Pray that the eyes of your understanding will be opened.
You have dual citizenship both here on
Earth and you have a presence in Heaven
Holy Spirit will Help you build your relationship and trust in Him who can only be seen through the eyes of a heart that yearns to understand.

He Sent His Angels

For centuries, our Army here in America has trained so effectively.
The members themselves have been transformed
into powerful weapons, as you can see.
An organized military force equipped and
trained for fighting on land,
But what about before Earth's time began?
What about in Eternity where God lives?

What we now see did not come from anything that can be seen.
Earth is simply a reflection of Heaven,
or at least it is supposed to be as Father God's original design.
He is the origin of everything seen and unseen
and He chooses to be invisible.
But does invisible mean it doesn't exist?
Of course not, because that would mean the air we breathe, the
thoughts we think, and the gravity that keeps us
grounded really don't exist,
they are just figments of our imagination, right?

You see God's original army which is an
Army of Angels who excel in great power,

there are Divisions upon divisions of Angels with special giftings
to help those who have inherited the promise of Salvation.

So Believer why do you entertain thoughts from the spirit of fear?
Do you know the address of where that spirit lives?
Don't you know who you are and that God
would never allow us to be left alone?
His army of Angels are always listening
for you to speak God's Word
in faith and to protect you.

Wherever you go, you have access to the Ruler of the Universe.
He won't let you down, that's not His style.
That's not how He operates.
Out of the Goodness of His Heart,
He has prepared a book of promises written just for
You that will activate His spiritual laws in your life and
bring Glory to His Name
each and every time you call on Him.

Angels enforce His Law but are neutralized
every time you speak words of
Doubt, Fear, or Worry
They won't pardon you for not believing God.
That's just not how this realm works.
But keep in mind one angel took out 185,000
who were against God's people in one night.
They excel in power, they can move faster than the speed of light.
They are with you right now (listening) to do good on your behalf
Can you even remember the last time you

spoke in your authority by faith?
Expecting the King to manifest His goodness
in response to you.

AS HE IS SO AM I

He gave you His Eternal Word and said speak as I Speak.
He gave you His Spirit and said have dominion
over the entire world.
He gave you the authority to use His Name and said,
"Everything will bow down to you according to your
faith in My Name."

The Angels will listen to you and go
forth when you speak My Word.
You can command His Blood in any situation and by faith that
circumstance has to Change. He even gave you the measure of
faith to use and it never fails.
God even commanded the Blessing of Abraham on you,
because the First Born lives inside you.

The Lord even put His Kingdom inside of you with access to
Heaven's inexhaustible supply.
He said to you, "Ask Me for anything
and whatever you can think of."
Or ask, "I can do exceedingly and abundantly
above what you desire."

Who are you that Almighty God would
bestow His power upon you and
say, "Imitate Me and share in My Power."

Praise Is A Weapon

Praise should be your instrument of choice.
It's not just something you do; You Are Praise.
Focus on The King of Glory like a laser… You play your
instrument of praise and allow
your mouth to speak forth what your heart is saying about Him.

It won't be long now…You will sense and discern His Presence
manifesting…
God is on His way…the atmosphere is shifting…
Praise even more...
But be cautious, there is something every
believer must realize but not
give too much attention.

You have an unseen enemy who is also a spirit.
He calls himself the prince of the air and he loves to
whisper lies in your ear.
Oh, he is conning, but only if you entertain the lies, He says.

He is not a god or even a King like our God
He is the father of all lies; A created thing.

And he is subject to the command of
every believer in Jesus.

So, as you lift your hands and give Praise
to the Lord, nothing else matters.
His precious Spirit dwells within your heart already
But as You Praise Him, He will make His
Awesome Presence known to You
He will live in Your Praise and make every
enemy of His and yours run.

So don't ever think you are alone or that you are a victim.
You don't have to go looking for God; Praise Him and
He will come to you.
Yes, God Almighty will make Himself known to you.
Don't be afraid of Our King

Praise is a mighty weapon.
It will set an atmosphere for
God Himself to come closer to you.
This is actually a guaranteed promise;
All you have to do is apply what you have
learned from the Word of God.

WHAT **I**S **Y**OUR **C**ONFESSION??

They searched for Jesus with all their hearts; without
a map they found Him.
Without a satellite signal, the Lord was found by them.
They found Him by Faith.

Jarius confessed that his daughter would be
healed and live if he could just find Jesus.
The woman with the issue of blood confessed
she would be made whole if she could only
touch the hem of His Garment.

Believe only what you have confessed by faith.
Don't be afraid it won't happen; the Lord
hears you, He always does.
Put your trust in God to perform His
Word that He gave to you.

The demand has been placed on the anointing.
Miracles are on the way.
You are now operating in God's Law of confession.

Let Jesus see your faith.
Confess every word to Him who lives forever.

<u>Your Scars Have Become Beauty</u>

Life can be painful; some pain can't be avoided.
But because of the Lord Jesus, everything you went through is now a Master Key to help someone else rise up and in the process of all the pain and anguish.
God made you who you were born to be; irresistibly beautiful, unstoppable, always abounding in Holy boldness.

This is G.R.A.C.E.
Now you have a story to tell that the world can't wait to hear
Now you have a testimony that shows forth
the Power of God at work in this natural realm
Now when people look at your life,
it will glorify God to the utmost.

Even Jesus learned obedience through the things he suffered
And out of His Life came the gift of Eternal life for all who believe in Him; and now out of your life, your struggle, your pain, your gift will make room for you.
Be as awesome as you dare to be and show the world that the King Of Glory lives by doing what looks impossible.

Eyes have not seen and ears have not heard
Nor has it entered into the heart, all the wonderful things you are about to do when you lean on and trust in the Lord.
Trusting in Him gives the illusion that you are vulnerable.
But take a closer and deeper look; there are more Angels with you than them in the world.

Your faith is only invisible to those who cannot see because they don't know the Spirit of the Living God.
He is with you and His power is limitless.
Rely only on what is written in His Word (The Bible) and what His precious Holy Spirit says to you.

Trust Him. Perfect love casts out all fears.
He will never leave you ashamed
Because that's not His nature or an image He wants to be attached to His Name
And He will always cause you to win; You can count on Him more than you trust yourself.

I speak from experience and now it's your turn
to see your mourning turned into dancing.
Now the scars you have acquired have stripped away all impurities.
Now the entire world can see Him who sent you.
Get Ready!

I Kissed You This Morning

I kissed you this morning and you didn't even know it.
I kissed you this morning and gave you
My very breath to breathe and not once today
did you acknowledge My Presence or ask
Me for help when you needed it most.
But I am always thinking of you,
whether it is in time or eternity.

I am a very patient Person, there is none like Me.
I have given you the opportunity for your spiritual
eyes to be opened to what reality
really is by simply believing in Me, but you still
refuse to see or understand My Perfect Ways.

After all, I made you in My image and My likeness. You are a speaking spirit as well, but since you can't see the spirit realm all around you, you think it must not be real.
Oh, but it's more real than you know and this realm affects your current life every day by the very authority of your own words.

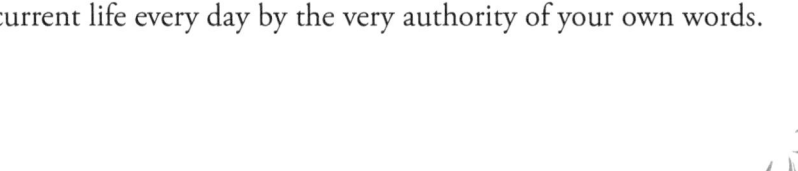

You rely too much on your own natural senses as if
this mere human life is all there is to live for.
But wait until you cross the path of one of
My faithful servants that I have sent to enlighten you.
Then as I the Lord, The God of Heaven's Armies,
your Unseen Partner lives and works "in" and "through"
them… I will reach past your soul to your spirit,
which is the real you. Then you shall finally understand,
then you will finally hear Me and see My Invisible Hand.

You will be filled with unspeakable
joy because you will Know Me.
I Am The Lord, your Unseen Partner,
There is none like Me because I love you.
I will continue to wait for you. So,
I will see you in the morning when I kiss you yet again.

<u>When God Whispers</u>

---❦---

The person who has ears to hear will hear whispers
from the Father.
He can speak to your spirit in a crowd full of
people and no one will know what He said but you. Write it
down, it's important. He can give you visions and dreams in the
middle of the night while your body and mind are at rest.

When you awake, write down what you saw,
it too is important.
He can download the spiritual truth you
need to know to prosper in the blink of an eye…
There is no one on Earth beyond His
reach and there is no one beyond
His power. You only need to draw near to
Him and He will draw near to you.

Believer in Christ Jesus, prepare yourselves.
Prepare your hearts as you enter into His Presence.
For I tell you that many prophets and kings wanted to see what
you see; But did not see it. And to hear
what you hear but did not hear it.

It is an honor and a privilege not given to
all to hear secrets from heaven.
But can He trust you with such
Greater things and revelation as this?
Can God trust you to do what is right even
when it's hard to do solely because it is precious to Him?

In the hard places of life will you be
obedient when you think no one is watching.
Know that God rewards you openly for the
things you have done in private.
This is the Goodness of God and He works in secret.

A Hurt That Only God Almighty Knows

You gave me this heart…
You created me in Your Image and Likeness.
Lord, You said guard your heart with all diligence
because out of it flows the issues of
Life, meaning according to my heart is how
I will see and deal with life.
And yet I don't know you Lord,
but I never meant to hurt You.

This heart that you gave me is like a garden's soil;
whatever gets planted by words or thoughts, grows.
As water reflects the face, so does my life reflect my heart.
So, what about when I don't want to read my Bible even though I
know this is good for my heart?
What about when I don't want to go to
Church and this is good for my heart?

Or when I'd rather not spend time in Prayer and this
too is very good for my heart.
But I never meant to hurt You, Lord. I promise I didn't.
So, what exactly is this heart you have given me,

and it rules over my life?
Is it what beats in my chest day and night?
Or is it actually my spirit and how I came to know and acknowledge You, Lord?

I now realize You are Who I have been searching for.
The emptiness in my heart was yearning for You.
Now I see. Yes, I need to know more about You and experience Your Awesome Presence.

I know I can't erase the pain I may have caused You my Lord but honestly, I didn't realize I was hurting your feelings.
I didn't mean to hurt You by not getting to know You and not being a willing vessel to reach other souls.
I truly repent and turn away from that life
I used to know. That empty life without You.

<u>To Be Blessed</u>

The Blessing of the Lord will make you rich and add no sorrow. The Blessing says, "May the Lord bless you and protect you; May the Lord smile on you and be gracious to you; May the Lord show you His Favor and Give you His Peace."

Imagine getting more out of life, God's way.
It can be so simple, but we tend to make a lot of things complex. How can you live an abundant life and become a true blessing to others just like Jesus?

There is a code in the Bible that teaches such things.
it is seen as a mystery. Nevertheless, it is still a code; an outline that can be followed by any Believer.

It will take a commitment and a dedicated heart to see God's plan for your life unfold. Are you willing to say Words about yourself that seem to be untrue at the moment?
Be misunderstood by almost everyone, persecuted, and even laughed at?

But when God looks at you, He says "You are the apple of My
Eye and an object of My Affection; Obedience to
Me is my love language."
Well, when you're ready, God never changes. He is the same
yesterday, today, and forevermore.

He wants you to prosper and be in good
health just as your soul prospers.
Just one Word from Him will change your
whole life but it will cost you a dedicated heart.
Are you sure you're ready??

Power of His Name

Throw away all of your fears.
All authority in the universe has been given to our King.
He has provided Salvation and Power to all who believe in Him.
As believers, you are now brothers and sisters of Christ Jesus
because we all have the same Father.

Jesus has supreme power and authority
over the invisible and visible Worlds.
He rules by the power of His Word and now so can you.
You must learn how to operate in the Kingdom of God.
You must build your faith in Him and His Word each day and
realize that it is no longer you who lives but
Christ now lives in you.

Faith is the required evidence used to prove what is still unseen.
You must be fully persuaded and convinced that the moment you
pray according to His Word, God hears you, and the promise
is on the way but there will also be spiritual warfare to try and
hinder what you believe God for and to try to make you doubt
His promises to you.

Take your stand. This is The Good Fight of faith which says even
when I don't see anything change around me at the moment.
I know what He promised me and He who promised is faithful.
Begin to give praise to the Messiah The Breaker. Make faith
declarations based on what you believe Him to do.

Make the declaration but look to Him to manifest the promise.
Jesus is still saying, "Do you believe I am able
to do what you are asking for?"
Holy Spirit show The Body Of Christ what
they can't see on their own
In Jesus Name we pray…

<u>Without A Cause</u>

How can you dislike someone you don't even know?
Is it because the words they speak are so full of
wisdom and power?
Or is it because of the way they carry themselves?

Doing good wherever that person goes.
They hated Jesus without a cause. He never hurt anyone.
Yet He kept right on doing the Father's will despite what people thought of Him.

Do you know when you say yes to Jesus the
same thing will happen to you?
Yes, You. You new creation in Christ Jesus; When you really want to know Jesus and His ways. Worldly people will turn on you which could even mean some of your family members or even some of your closest friends.

But take note, it is not the people themselves you are wrestling with but against powers, against rulers of darkness, and against spiritual wickedness in high places influencing them. You see you have been marked in the spirit realm by the Lord Jesus.

You belong to Him now; You were bought with a price.

God gave His life in exchange for yours.
So, we wouldn't have to spend eternity without Him which is eternal outer darkness… So, the least you could do is spend some quality time each day with the person who died for you to live and be blessed.

Read about His amazing love for you in His Word.
Open the book and see what you have been missing.
Understand His power. Get to know Him. Invite His Wisdom.
Let your eyes be open and have ears to hear His lovely voice.

This is your divine birthright.

WHY SHOULD THE **M**EEK **I**NHERIT

---❦---

Meekness says I am nothing yet because of Him, I am everything.
I own nothing yet everything is at my disposal.
I listen carefully to the words that come from men's hearts.
This exposes who they truly are but still, I walk in peace.

I pursue peace at all costs except when my peace is disturbed,
then war is on the Horizon.
I can remain calm in all situations because
I know God will fight for me.
The question is, do you believe when you pray that at that very
moment, you have received what you asked God for?

Nothing seemed to change in the natural
realm around you at that second.
There was no tingly feelings or flashing lights that indicated the
change you asked for was happening

His written word is all you need and the Holy Spirit will confirm
to you whatever is necessary at that time.
You have to learn to walk in the Spirit of God and as your faith in
Him and His Word grows, miracles will break forth in your life.

It can be no other way because He only does wondrous things.
He is the God of the Miraculous.

You see, believers who have big faith in Him are called Sons of God and they are truly the meek and do the Father's Will.
They will inherit the Earth because it has been promised to them.
God never lies nor does He need to repent from the Words He has already spoken.
You can trust Him with your life.

WHAT HAPPENED AT THE CROSS

There was no hope in this lifetime if Jesus had not come.
God Almighty decided He was not going to live an eternity
without you and I.
The King and His Kingdom came to reside
on the inside of every Believer.

This is the mystery. This is the enigma that
the world can't understand.
How can the God of the Universe live on the inside of each and
every person that invites Him in to dwell?

It is written that we are fearfully and wonderfully made.
God knows the end before the beginning ever started.
God designed us in such a way that He could have an intimate
relationship with us, uninterrupted.

You may not feel any different, and you may not look any
different, but you certainly are. The only limitation you have
now is not hearing His Voice clearly as you should because of all
the distractions surrounding you. At the cross, Jesus put evil in

its proper place and snatched mankind out of the kingdom of darkness and what He accomplished can never be undone.

The end of this age as we know is approaching rapidly.
A New Order is replacing life as we once knew it.
The Cross gave every human being on the planet a decision to make about Jesus and this decision will determine where you will spend your eternity.

Have you seriously taken the time to really evaluate what your life is all about?

Responses To The Finished Works

Hope deferred can hurt my heart.
I trust you God, but why am I not seeing the manifestation of
God's goodness in my life?
Why does my life resemble the world?

But God You said I am in this world but not of this world.
I received Christ in my heart.
I read the bible and pray quite a bit.
I can sense His nearness every day, but why am I
not experiencing this New Creation life?
Where am I missing it? Where is this new life that My Lord
promised me and my family?

Then I heard in my spirit one day as I prayed.
Are you applying what you learned from the Word of God or just
reading the Bible as a mere book?
Are you hungry for a change in your life?

Good Godly change will require that you
ask Me nothing if your heart is full of doubt.

Ask Me nothing if you doubt if I can hear you when you pray,
you should keep quiet.
Ask Me nothing If you doubt I will answer you
when you call on Me, another reason to keep silent.

I will not respond to doubt or fear.
And if you doubt that The Great 'I AM" can change your life in
the blink of an eye, just keep quiet.
Your prayers never went past your ceiling.

I tell you the Truth I can see your faith before you even speak.
I can smell your prayers as they come before Me and the very
reason I laid down My life for you is because I long to be
everything you would ever need in life.
I have given you My Son. I have given you
My Word and I have even given you the
measure of faith to use.
If this isn't enough for you to believe Me,
then tell Me what is?

<u>I Am A Witness</u>

---❦---

My life testifies that I know Him…Him Who…
The Great I Am…
The One Who died but now lives forever.
When you look at me; you see Him.
I talk like Him; God's Word is my vocabulary.
I walk like Him; His Holy Spirit orders my
every step and even if I make a mistake.
He always turns It for my good.

I am fearfully and wonderfully made in His Image and likeness. Miracles, signs, and wonders follow me all the days of my life, and they bear witness to the truth that Jesus has authority on this Earth and He lives in me.

Jesus said that "If you don't see miracles in My life, don't believe Me" and we too should also say, "If you don't see Miracles in my life, don't believe anything I say."
Can you be that bold?
Bold enough to live off the promises
of God while still working at your current job?
Trusting Him for increase.

Trusting Him for peace in a world
that seems turned upside down.
And trusting Him to restore everything
that has been stolen from you and your
family by the enemy knowingly and unknowingly.

Can you live by what is unseen?
Can you live by faith in the midst of whatever is going on?
That's the question every Believer has to answer.
Can you trust Jesus even when you can't trace Him?

<u>It Is Finished</u>

---❦---

Forever, Oh Lord Your Word is settled in Heaven.
Your Word is law; higher than all man's natural
laws in this World.
Jesus said 'It is finished',
now Heaven and Earth are again connected as one.

As Believers, we can bind on Earth what
is already forbidden in Heaven.
And we can release on the Earth
only what is permitted in Heaven.
This Earth shall resemble Heaven again
under the ruling authority and
power that Jesus has given us.

Don't be afraid that you are different; peculiar even.
God is with you right now, protecting you and guiding you no
matter what it looks like or how you feel.

Speak His Word only; The Angels of God are
listening and so is the enemy.
God is always watching over His Word.

He never sleeps or slumbers.
He is His Word…So, how can He deny Himself?
He will never fail you, let you down,
or allow you to be ashamed because you believed in Him.

He desires to bless you and show you His goodness.
He is faithful even when you are not..
It is finished means you have partnered with
the invisible realm of God. You only need to
renew your mind so you begin to think like Him.
Reading the Word of God is a necessity
and declaring His Word in faith is your new life.
"IT IS Finished"

WHAT IS **P**RAYER??

All powerful God we thank You right now that
You always hear us when we pray
according to Your Word.
Where is Your Glory? Let Your Glory come forth in full Power.
I know that You are everywhere.

At the same time, let our prayers come before Your Throne of
Grace with a sweet aroma. Thank You for answers coming forth
from the Courts of Heaven
that will manifest Your perfect Will in our lives.

Prayer is a conversation with God
where we both listen to each other.
But ultimately, He already knows what
we have need of before we even ask.
Prayer is bringing Heaven to Earth.
Your Kingdom come Your Will be done on
Earth as it is in Heaven.

Little prayer life equals little power here on this Earth.
Prayer is reminding God of the promises He made to you.

By faith, it creates an atmosphere for
God to show up on your behalf.

Fight on your behalf and give you wisdom
beyond what the world can understand.
It opens the doors to do the supernatural.
Prayer is partnering with God the Holy Spirit to know His Heart
and call forth deliverance and divine strategy.

Make time for prayer every day.
It will change you on the inside first and then it will change your
outside surroundings. Your words are more than just sound.
Your words are meant to create your reality.

God never works alone.
So if you thought you were waiting on Him,
He is actually waiting on you.

Why Should I Pour Out My Heart To The Lord

My prayers crack Heaven wide open.
There is a Holy rage inside me for Justice to
be served here on Earth.
Iron sharpens Iron, but who really is my brother?
God hears me but my faith is being tested.

I will endure these trials in perfect peace because I know God is
with me and He alone will rescue.
He is the Hope of my life.
Maturity comes from trusting Him when it
seems trouble is on every side.

I can't trace Him but I know Him for myself in my heart.
He Who promised is faithful.
He is good to me and He will never allow me to be ashamed for
believing in Jesus.

The enemy may be whispering "That you're done."
But the peace in my heart says I have just begun to
manifest His Glory.

Even when I am tired, I will never grow
weary of doing what is good.

Remember me My Lord and have mercy on me.
My life is but a vapor and has no meaning without You.
We serve a wonderful God who will wipe away every tear we have
cried and comfort us.

We are fully persuaded it can be no other way.
Our God is unable to fail. His nature is to bless and prosper us.
When we pray from our heart, we receive His grace.

What Does It Look Like to Operate in the Finished Works

My Name is Worship…
My address is Victory…
My voice is praise…
I enter a room and the atmosphere shifts…
I live to be in His Presence…
I hunger for His every Word
As a result my words have become a two-edged sword
I hear secrets from Heaven
My dreams are more real than the natural world itself
I can see things play out before they ever happen
My faith can breakthrough any confinement
I live only to do His Will.. This truly pleases me
Jesus is my King… The One who loves me when no one else seems to care
He is the One Who won my victory…
I owe Him Everything….
My obedience to Him is all that I have to give
I pray that it is enough….

www.ingramcontent.com/pod-product-compliance
Lightning Source LLC
Chambersburg PA
CBHW041235060526
44107CB00136BA/725